The Award
WORLD ATLAS

Published by Award Publications Limited
Spring House, Spring Place
London NW5
Printed in Belgium

The Award
WORLD ATLAS

CONTENTS

AWARD PUBLICATIONS – LONDON

ENGLAND and WALES—PHYSICAL

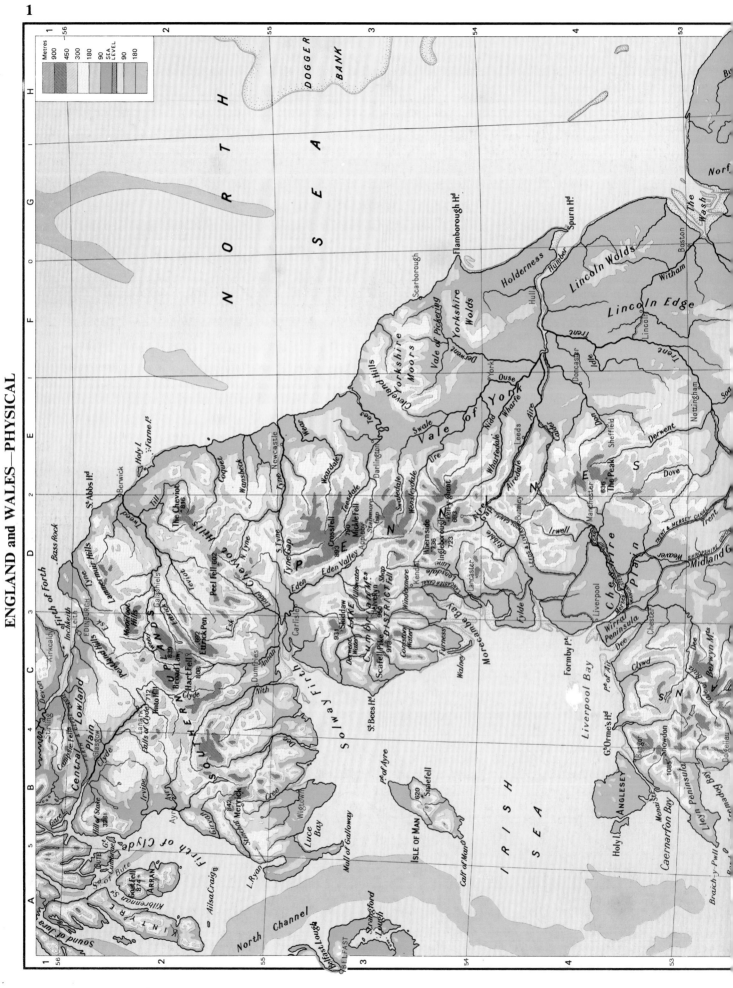

Metres
900
450
300
180
90
SEA LEVEL
90
180

N O R T H   S E A

DOGGER BANK

Norf

The Wash

Boston

Witham

Spurn Hd

Humber

Hull

Holderness

Lincoln Wolds

Lincoln Edge

Lincoln

Trent

Idle

Trent

Doncaster

Don

Sheffield

Nottingham

Derwent

Dove

The Peak

636

MIDLAND G

Weaver

TRENT & MERSEY CANAL

SHROPSHIRE UNION

Chester

Dee

Clwyd

Dee

Berwyn Mts

Flamborough Hd

Scarborough

Vale of Pickering

Yorkshire Wolds

Derwent

Cleveland Hills

North Yorkshire Moors

Vale of York

Ouse

York

Aire

Nidd

Wharfe

Leeds

Wharfedale

Airedale

Nidderdale

Calder

Burnley

Irwell

Manchester

MANCHESTER SHIP CANAL

Liverpool

Cheshire Plain

Wirral Peninsula

Pt. of Air

Liverpool Bay

Formby Pt.

Gt. Orme's Hd

Bangor

Menai Str.

ANGLESEY

Holy I.

Snowdon
1085

Caernarfon Bay

Llyn Peninsula

Braich-y-Pwll

Bardsey I.

S N O

Dodell

Swale

Teesdale

Ure

Wensleydale

Swaledale

Ribble

P E N N I N E S

Whernside
736

Ingleborough
723

Lune

Lancaster

Lunesdale

LANCASTER CANAL

Fylde

Morecambe Bay

Furness

Walney

Kendal

Windermere

Coniston Water

St. Bees Hd

Scafell Pike
978

Derwent Water

Helvellyn
950

Ullswater

LAKE DISTRICT

CUMBRIAN Mts

Skiddaw
931

Shap

Shap Fell

Eden Valley

Cross Fell
893

Mickle Fell
790

Appleby

Stainmore

Darlington

Tees

S. Tyne

Eden

Carlisle

Solway Firth

Dumfries

Nith

Cree

Esk

Annan

N. Tyne

Tyne Gap

Peel Fell
602

CHEVIOT HILLS

The Cheviot
816

Coquet

Wansbeck

Newcastle

Wear

Weardale

Tyne

Holy I.

Farne Is.

Berwick

Till

Tweed

St. Abbs Hd

Teviot

Lammermuir Hills

Tyne Hills

Moorfoot Hills

Galashiels

SOUTHERN UPLANDS

Broad Law
839

Ettrick

Ettrick Pen
692

Hart Fell
808

Tinto Hill 712

Lanark

Falls of Clyde

EDINBURGH

Leith

Esk

Inchkeith

Firth of Forth

Kirkcaldy

Dunfermline

Devon

Stirling

Campsie Fells

Kilpatrick Hills

Clyde

Glasgow

Central Lowland

Irvine

Ayr

Girvan

Clyde

Hill of Stake
388

Nith

Sanquhar

Merrick
842

Wigtown

Luce Bay

Mull of Galloway

Wigtown Bay

Dee

L. Ryan

Ailsa Craig

Firth of Clyde

Goatfell
874

ARRAN

Kilbrennan Sd.

Sound of Bute

KINTYRE

Sound of Jura

Gt. Cumbrae

Sd. of

Sr. of

Garr

North Channel

Strangford Lough

Belfast Lough

BELFAST

Pt. of Ayre

ISLE OF MAN

620
Snaefell

Calf of Man

I R I S H   S E A

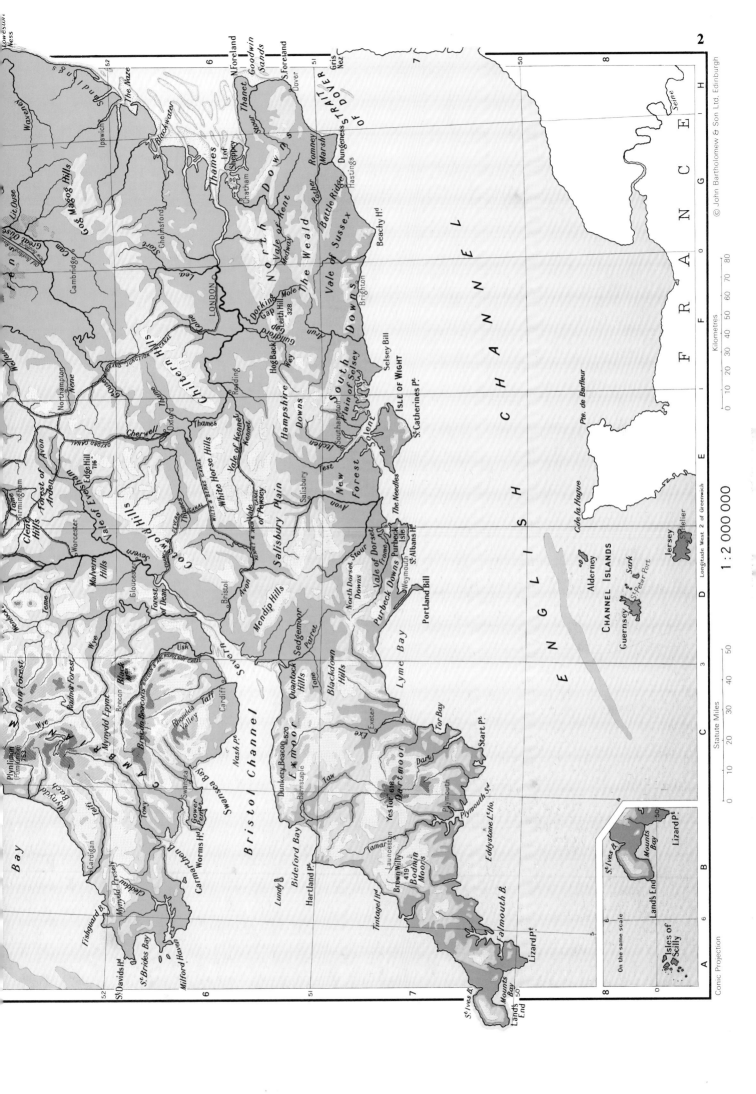

ENGLAND and WALES—POLITICAL

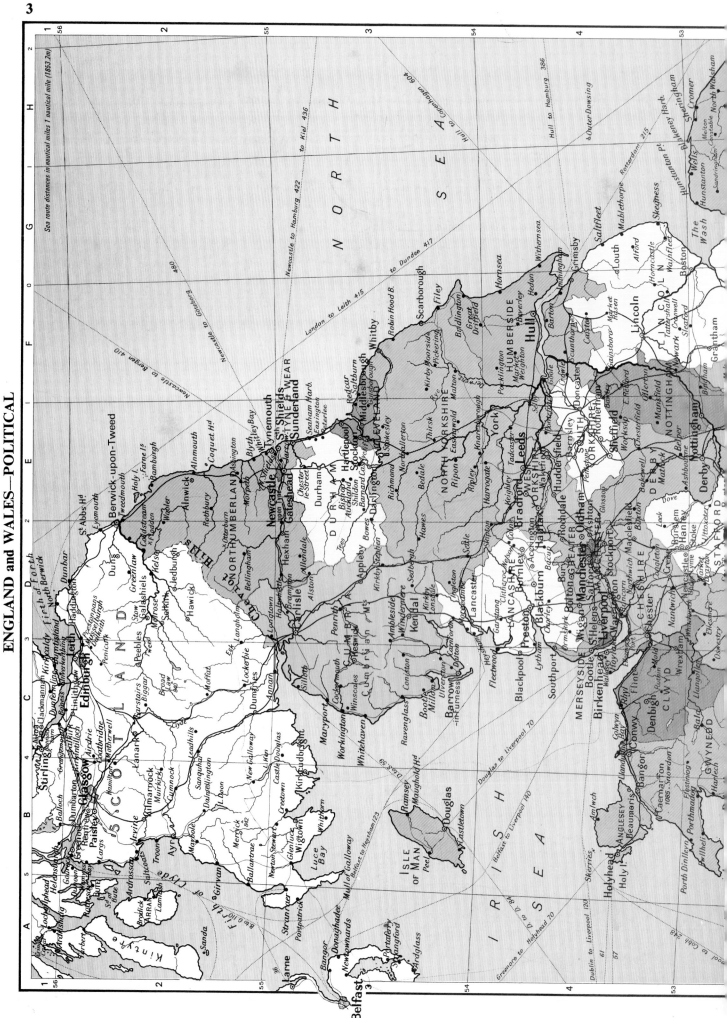

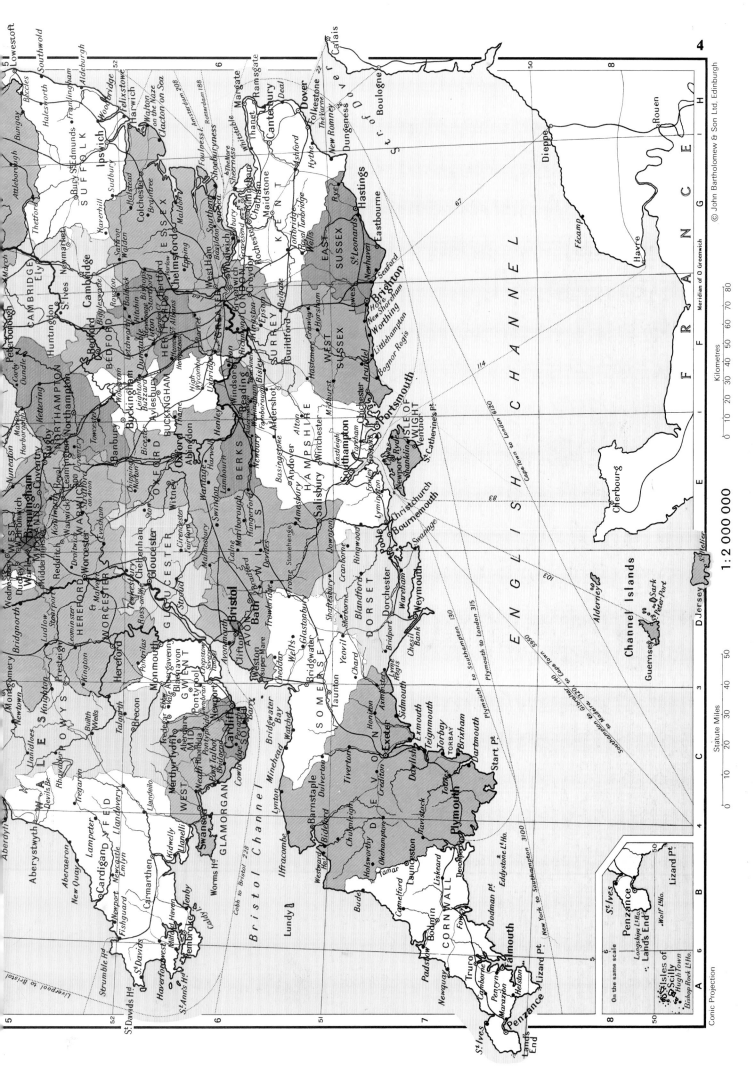

Metres
900
450
300
180
90
SEA LEVEL
90
180

SHETLAND ISLANDS

Unst
Yell
Fetlar
St Magnus Bay
Papa Stour
Whalsa
Lerwick
Bressay
Sumburgh Hd
60

ORKNEY ISLANDS
Nth Ronaldsay
Papa Westray
Westray
Sanday
Rousay
Shapinsay
Kirkwall
Scapa Flow
Burray
Sth Ronaldsay
Duncansby Hd
Pentland Firth
Old Man of Hoy
Hoy

N. Rona
Sula Sgier
Sule Skerry
Stack Skerry

Cape Wrath
L. Eriboll
Kyle of Tongue
Strathy Pt
Dunnet Hd
Dunnet
Thurso
Sinclairs B.
Noss Hd
Wick

Butt of Lewis
Flannan Is
LEWIS
Stornoway
Scarp
Taransay
Clisham 799
HARRIS
Sound of Harris
Pabbay
N. Uist
Benbecula
Ben More 620 S. Uist
Barra
Barra Hd

North Minch
Little Minch
Shiant Is
Loch Ewe
Gair Loch
Loch Torridon
Rona
Raasay
SKYE
L. Snizort
Storr
Cuillin Hills
Cuillin
Canna
L. Scavaig
Rum
Eigg
Muck
Oigh-sgeir

Eddrachillis Bay
Foinaven 908
Ben Hope 927
L. Loyal
L. Naver
Ben Hee 873
Ben Klibreck 961
Morven 705
Enard Bay
Eas-Coul-Aulin Falls
Ben More Assynt 1027
Suilven 731
Loch Shin
S. Oykel
Dornoch
Dornoch Firth
Tarbat Ness
Cromarty Firth
Moray Firth

Gruinard B.
Loch Broom
Falls of Measach
Ben Dearg 1087
Slioch 994
L. Maree
L. Fannich
Ben Wyvis 1045
Black Isle
Beauly
Inverness
Nairn
Findhorn
Elgin
Culbin Forest
Banff
Deveron
Kinnairds Head
Rattray Hd
Peterhead
Buchan Ness
Ythan

L. Monar
L. Alsh
Glen Affric 1177
Mam Soul 1031
Ben Attow
Glen Moriston
Meall Fuar-vounie 696
Loch Ness
Falls of Foyers
Monadhliath Mts
Cairngorms 1293
Ben Macdui 1309
Cairn Toul
Carn Mor 803
Morven 872
Hill of Fare 471
Dee
Girdle Ness
Aberdeen
Don
Braemar

Knoydart
Glen Garry
L. Oich
Corrieyairack
L. Laggan
Ben Alder 1145
Drumochter Pass
Ben Dearg 1007
Glen Garry
Ben-y-Gloe 1119
Lochnagar 1154
Glas Maol 1067
Battock 779
N. Esk
Mearns

L. Morar
L. Arkaig
L. Lochy
Ben Nevis 1344
Fort William
L. Eil
L. Shiel
Sunart
L. Linnhe
L. Leven
Glen Coe
L. Etive
Ben Cruachan 1124
Oban
Loch Awe

Ardnamurchan Pt
Coll
Tiree
Staffa
Iona
MULL
Ben More 966
Morvern
Mull
Firth of Lorn

Ranmoch Moor
Schiehallion 1081
Ben Lawers 1214
L. Tay
L. Rannoch
Tummel
Pass of Killiecrankie
Strath more
Sidlaw Hills
Dundee
Buddon Ness
Bell Rock
Carse of Gowrie
F. of Tay
Perth
Almond
L. Earn
Ben More 1171
Ben Luie 1130
L. Katrine
Ben Vorlich 983
Trossachs 973
Carn Hills
Ben Lomond
L. Lomond
Ochil Hills
Howe of Fife Eden
Lomond Hills
Fife Ness
L. of May
L. Leven
Kirkcaldy
Firth of Forth
Bass Rock
Inchkeith
Leith
St Abb's Hd

GRAMPIAN MOUNTAINS
GREAT GLEN
WESTERN HIGHLANDS

Jura
Raps of Jura 784
Sound of Jura
Str. of Corryvreckan
Colonsay
Dubh Artach
Skerryvore
ISLAY
Sound of Islay
Gigha
Mull of Oa
Kilbrennan Sd
Goat Fell 874
ARRAN
Bute
Gt Cumbrae
Hill of Stake 522
KINTYRE
Firth of Clyde
Glasgow
Lanark
Falls of Clyde 712
Pentland Hills
Eddleston
Esk
Tyne
Lammermuir Hills
Berwick
Holy I.
Farne
The Merse
Tweed
Galashiels
Moorfoot Hills
EDINBURGH
Clyde
Campsie Fells
Central Lowlands
Stirling
Forth
Teith
Devon

Inishtrahull
Giant's Causeway
Rathlin I.
Fair Hd
Mull of Kintyre
Ailsa Craig
Irvine
Ayr
Ayr
Girvan
Pinto Hill 748
Broad Law 839
Culter 748
Tweedsmuir Hills
Leadhills
Lowther 732
Hart Fell 808
Ettrick Pen 692
St Marys L.
Ettrick
Teviotdale
Teviot
Hawick
The Cheviot 816
Peel Fell 602
Coquet
Wansbeck
N. Tyne
CHEVIOT HILLS
SOUTHERN UPLANDS
Nithsdale
Carsphairn 796
Cairnsmore
Merrick 842
Kells Range
L. Doon
Stinchar
L. Ryan
Galloway
L. Ken
L. Cree
Dee
Wigtown
Luce Bay
Mull of Galloway
Criffel 569
Dumfries
Annandale
Annan
Liddesdale
Liddel
Eden
Esk
Carlisle
Sth Tyne
Tyne
Tyne Gap
Newcastle

Inishowen
Lough Foyle
Derry
Coleraine
Bann
Plateau of Antrim
Trostan 554
Garron Pt
Sperrin Mts
Sawel Mt.

ATLANTIC OCEAN
NORTH SEA
OUTER HEBRIDES
NORTH CHANNEL

Conic Projection

Statute Miles
0 10 20 30 40

1 : 2 000 000

Kilometres
0 10 20 30 40 50 60 70

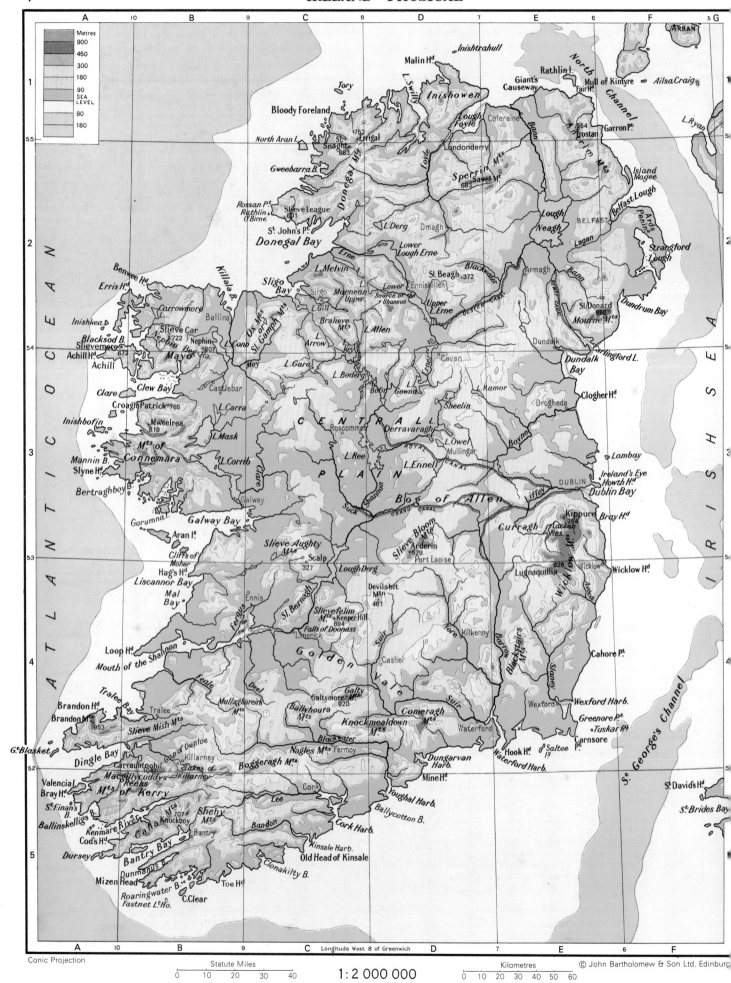

Conic Projection

Longitude West 8 of Greenwich

Statute Miles
0 10 20 30 40

1 : 2 000 000

Kilometres
0 10 20 30 40 50 60

© John Bartholomew & Son Ltd, Edinburgh

route distances in nautical miles, 1 nautical mile (1853.2m)

1 : 2,000,000

Statute Miles
0   10   20   30   40   50

Kilometres
0 10 20 30 40 50 60 70 80

© — John Bartholomew & Son.Ltd.Edinburgh

Longitude West 8 of Greenwich

Lambert's Zenithal Equal Area Projection

Statute Miles

1 : 18 000 000

Kilometres

N.B. While the Ural Mountains form the
traditional boundary of Europe, it is more
convenient to treat U.S.S.R. as in Eurasia.

Lambert's Zenithal Equal Area Projection

Statute Miles

1 : 45 000 000

Kilometres

© John Bartholomew & Son Ltd. Edinburgh

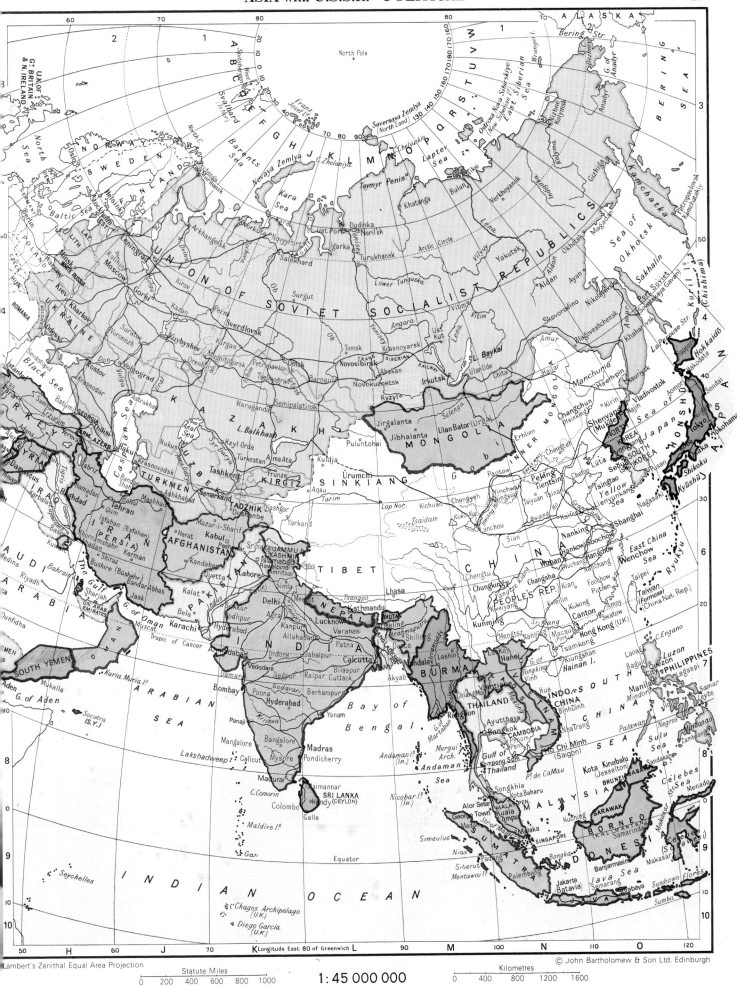

Lambert's Zenithal Equal Area Projection

Statute Miles
0   200   400   600   800 1000

Kilometres
0   400   800   1200 1600

1:45 000 000

© John Bartholomew & Son Ltd, Edinburgh

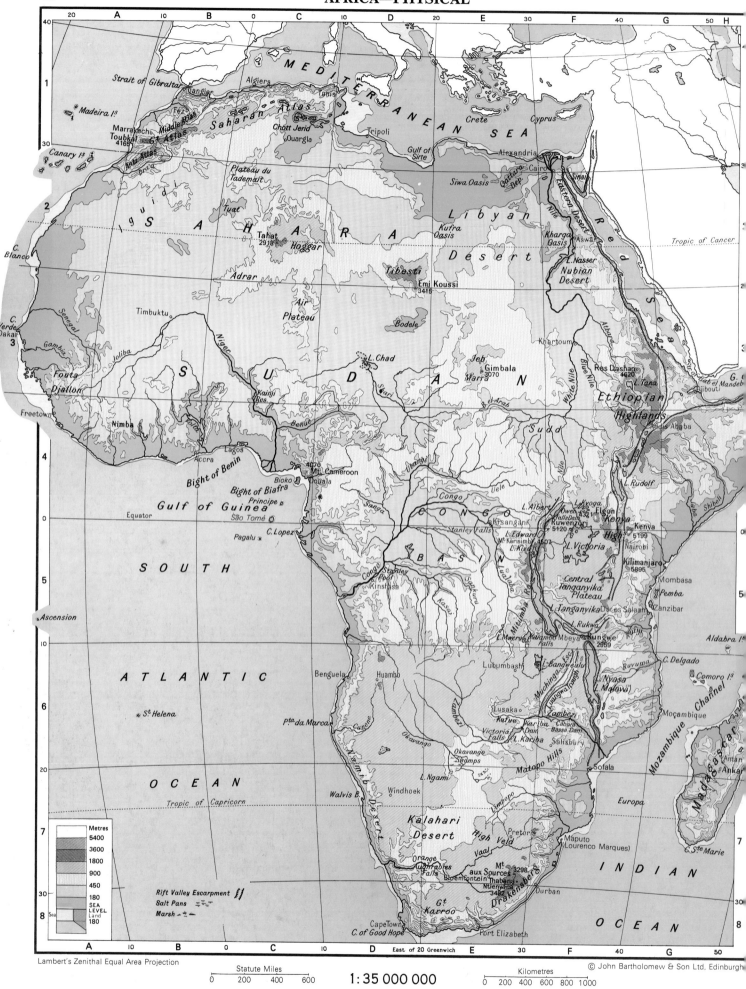

Lambert's Zenithal Equal Area Projection

Statute Miles

0   200   400   600

1 : 35 000 000

Kilometres

0   200 400 600 800 1000

Map labels

MEDITERRANEAN SEA

Strait of Gibraltar
Tangier
Algiers
Tunis
Crete
Cyprus
Madeira Is.
Fez
Saharan Atlas
Chott Jerid
Tripoli
Marrakech
Middle Atlas
Gt Atlas
Toubkal 4165
Ouargla
Gulf of Sirte
Anti Atlas
Canary Is.
pr d'a
Alexandria
Cairo
Plateau du Tademait
Siwa Oasis
Qattara Dep.
Sinai
Libyan
Nile
Eastern Desert
C. Blanco
S A H A R A
Tuat
Tahat 2918
Hoggar
Kufra Oasis
Desert
Tropic of Cancer
Kharga Oasis
Aswân
L. Nasser
Nubian Desert
Adrar
Tibesti
Emi Koussi 3415
Red Sea
C. Verde
Dakar
Air Plateau
Bodele
Khartoum
Ras Dashan 4620
Bab el Mandeb
Senegal
Timbuktu
Niger
L. Chad
Jeb. Gimbala 3070
White Nile
Blue Nile
Atbara
L. Tana
Djibouti
Gambia
Joliba
S U D A N
Jeb. Marra
Ethiopian Highlands
Fouta Djallon
Kainji Res.
Shari
Addis Ababa
Freetown
Benue
el Arab
Sudd
Nimba
Volta
Lagos
Accra
Mt. Cameroon 4070
Bioko
Douala
Ubangi
Shibeli
Bight of Benin
Bight of Biafra
Principe
Sanga
Uele
Congo
L. Albert
L. Kyoga
Elgon 4321
L. Rudolf
Gulf of Guinea
São Tomé
Kisangani
Owen Falls Dam
Ruwenzori 5120
Kenya High.
Kenya 5199
Equator
Stanley Falls
L. Edward
Mt Karisimbi 4507
L. Kivu
L. Victoria
Nairobi
Pagalu
C. Lopez
C O N G O
Kilimanjaro 5895
S O U T H
B A S I N
Lualaba
Central Tanganyika Plateau
Mombasa
Congo
Stanley Pool
Kinshasa
Kasai
Kwilu
L. Tanganyika
Dar es Salaam
Pemba
Zanzibar
A T L A N T I C
L. Mweru
Kalambo Falls
L. Rukwa
Ascension
Mitumba
Mbeya
Rungwe 2959
Aldabra Is.
L. Bangweulu
Ruvuma
C. Delgado
Benguela
Huambo
Lubumbashi
Muchinga
Luangwa Trough
L. Nyasa (L. Malawi)
Comoro Is.
O C E A N
Zambezi
Lusaka
Mozambique Channel
St. Helena
Kafue
Kariba Dam
Cabora Bassa Dam
Moçambique
Pta da Marca
Cunene
Victoria Falls
L. Kariba
Salisbury
Sofala
Okavango
Zambezi
Okavango Swamps
Matopo Hills
Namib Desert
L. Ngami
Windhoek
Limpopo
Europa
Tropic of Capricorn
Walvis B.
Madagascar
Antan.
Kalahari Desert
High Veld
Pretoria
Ankar.
Maputo (Lourenço Marques)
C. Ste Marie
Orange
Augrabies Falls
Mt aux Sources 3298
Thabana Ntlenyana 3482
INDIAN
Vaal
Bloemfontein
Drakensberg
Durban
Gt Karroo
Port Elizabeth
Cape Town
C. of Good Hope
O C E A N

Legend

Metres
5400
3600
1800
900
450
180
SEA LEVEL Land
Sea 180

Rift Valley Escarpment
Salt Pans
Marsh

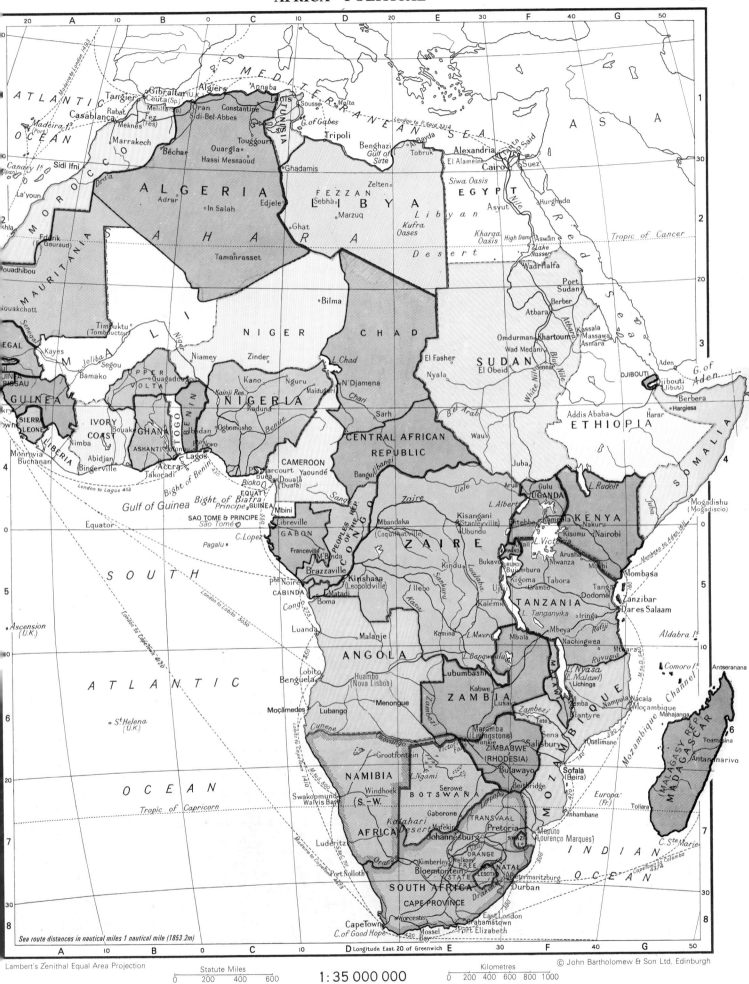

Lambert's Zenithal Equal Area Projection

Statute Miles
0   200   400   600

Sea route distances in nautical miles 1 nautical mile (1853.2m)

1:35 000 000

Kilometres
0 200 400 600 800 1000

© John Bartholomew & Son Ltd, Edinburgh

NORTH AMERICA—PHYSICAL

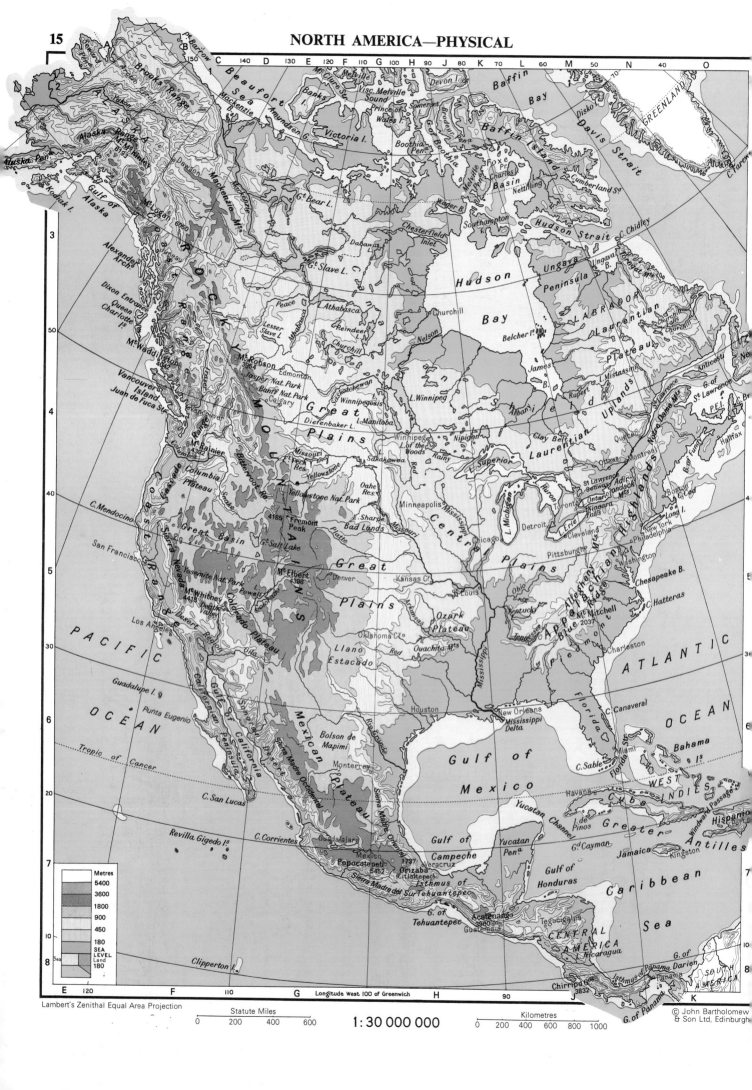

Metres
5400
3600
1800
900
450
180
SEA LEVEL
Land
180

Lambert's Zenithal Equal Area Projection

Statute Miles
0   200   400   600

1 : 30 000 000

Kilometres
0   200 400 600 800 1000

Longitude West 100 of Greenwich

© John Bartholomew & Son Ltd, Edinburgh

Lambert's Zenithal Equal Area Projection

Statute Miles
0   200   400   600

1 : 30 000 000

Kilometres
0   200   400   600   800   1000

© John Bartholomew & Son Ltd, Edinburgh

B 80 C 70 D 60 E 50 F 40 G

NORTH ATLANTIC OCEAN

P.ta Gallinas
Curaçao
Margarita
Tobago
Trinidad
Cristobal Colón 5775
Gulf of Darien
L. Maracaibo
Caracas
Georgetown
Paramaribo
Cayenne
C. Orange
Isthmus of Panama
G. of Panama
Malpelo
Cauca
Magdalena
Bogotá
Meta
Orinoco
Angel Falls
Roraima 2810
Kaieteur Falls
Guiana Highlands
Tolima 5215
Huila 5750
Guaviare
Orinoco
Casiquiare
Duida 2470
P.ta Galera
Quito
Cotopaxi 5896
Chimborazo 6267
Putumayo
Japurá
Negro
Amazon
Manaus
Amazon
Mouths of the Amazon
I. de Marajo
Belém (Pará)
Equator
Guayaquil
G. of Guayaquil
C. Blanco
Marañon
Ucayali
Juruá
Purus
S e l v a s
Tapajos
Xingu
Tocantins
Parnaiba
C. S. Ro
P.ta Aguja
Huascaran 6768
Lima
Madre de Dios
Madeira
Roosevelt
Araguaia
Catingas
Reci
Pern
Beni
Mamore
Guapore
Mato Grosso
Cercados
Francisco
Salvador (Bahia)
Corupuna 6425
Titicaca
Illampu 6485
C. Ancohuma 7014
Illimani 6882
La Paz
Sajama 6520
Bolivian Plateau
L. Poopo
Sucre
Bananal
Campos
Brasilia
Itambe 2033
Brazilian Highlands
Arica
Atacama Desert
Ollague 5860
Pilcomayo
Gran Chaco
Bermejo
Rio Grande
Itatiaia 2787
Sao Paulo
C. frio
Rio de Janeiro
PACIFIC
Tropic of Capricorn
Antofagasta
Llullaillaco 6723
Cerro Ojos del Salado 6908
Toro 6379
Paraguay
Paraná
Asuncion
Guaira Falls
Iguassu Falls
S. Felix
S. Ambrosio
Mar Chiquita
Uruguay
Salado
Lagoa dos Patos
OCEAN
Mercedario 6770
Aconcagua 6960
Valparaiso
Uspallata P.
Santiago
Alvarado P.
Maipo 5323
Rosario
Buenos Aires
Montevideo
La Plata
SOUTH ATLANTIC OCEAN
Juan Fernandez I.
P a m p a s
Lagoa Mirim
Lanin 3776
Colorado
Negro
Bahia Blanca
S.
L. Nahuel Huapi
Tronador 3554
G. San Matias
Valdes Pen.
Chiloe I.
Chubut
Chonos Archipelago
San Valentin 4058
G. San Jorge
Taitao Pen.
Patagonian Desert
Piramide 3380
Gt. Wellington I.
Bahia Grande
Falkland Is.
Str. of Magellan
Str. of Magellan
Punta Arenas
Tierra del Fuego
C. Horn

Metres
5400
3600
1800
900
450
180
SEA LEVEL
180
50

A 90 B 80 C 70 D 60 E West of 50 Greenwich F 40 G 30 H

Lambert's Zenithal Equal Area Projection

Statute Miles
0 200 400 600
1 : 30 000 000
Kilometres
0 200 400 600 800 1000

© John Bartholomew & Son Ltd., Edinburgh

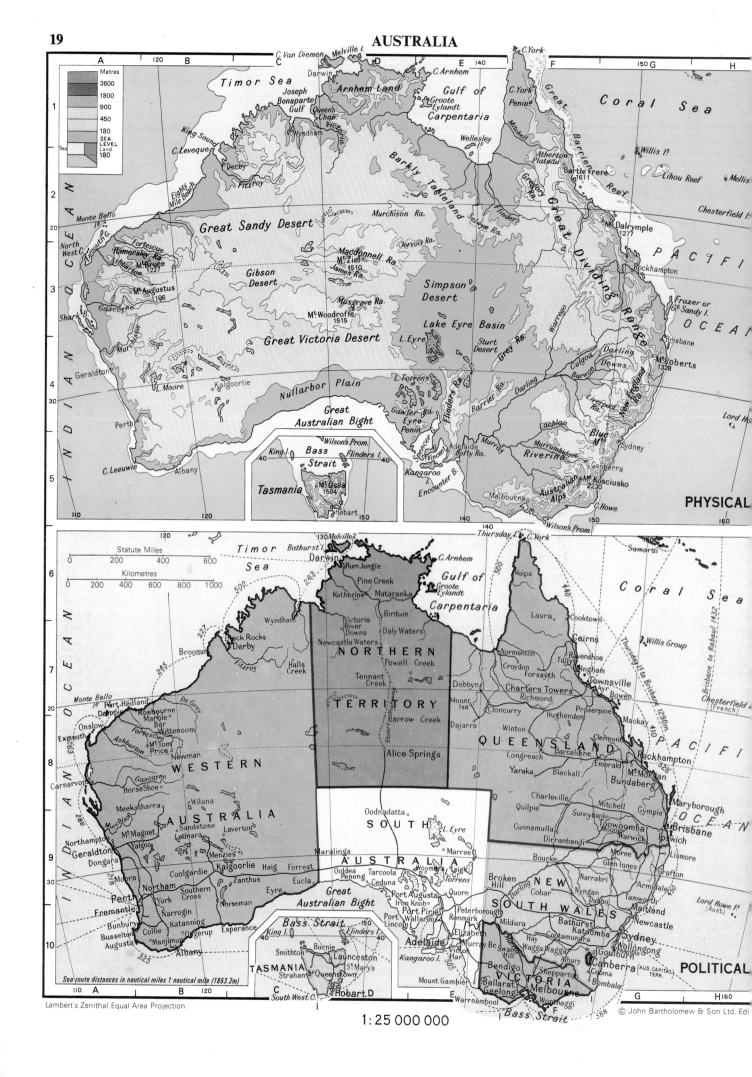

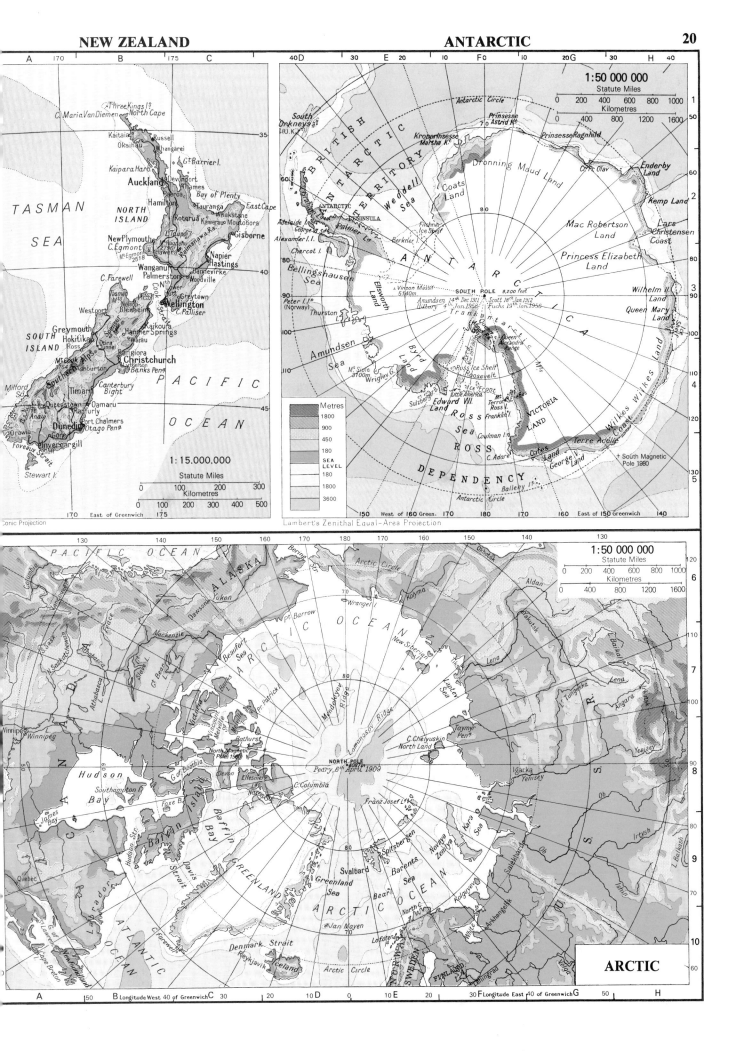

ARCTIC OCEAN

Laptev
Sea

C.Chelyuskin

Taymyr Peninsula

Ostrova Novo
Sibirskiye

Kotelnyy

Novaya Sibir

East Siberian

Sea

Taymyr

Igarka

Chukotsk
Sea

Wrangel I.

Beaufort
Sea

Pt Barrow

Mackenzie King I.
Pr.Patrick I.

Borden I.

Islands

Pr Albert
Pen.
Banks

Viscou
Melvi
Sd.

McClure Str.

Amundsen Gulf

Victori

Pr of Wales

U.S.A

Aklavik

Coppermine

Lower Tunguska

Verkhoyansk

Indigirka

Nizhne Kolymsk

Anadyr

Kolyma

Bering Str.

ALASKA

Yukon
Fairbanks

Dawson

NORTHWEST T

Yellowknife
Gt Slave

Ft Smith

Port Radium
Gt Bear L.

MACKENZIE
DIST.

Yenisey

Yakutsk

UNION of SOVIET SOCIALIST REPUBLICS

Lena

Yana

Gizhiga

Magadan

Okhotsk

Kamchatka

Bering Sea

Komandorskiye

St Lawrence I.

Nome

Anchorage

YUKON
TERRITORY

Novosibirsk

Krasnoyarsk

Ust'Kut

Lena-Kirensk

Sea of
Okhotsk

Nikolayevsk

Seward

Gulf of
Alaska

Juneau

Sitka

BRITISH
COLUMBIA

CA

Omsk
Tomsk

L.Balkash

Baikal
Chita
Yakhta

Komsomolsk

Blagoveshchensk

Petropavlovsk

Kiska I.

Dutch Harb.

Unalaska

Aleutian Is.

Kodiak I.

Pr.Rupert

ALBERTA

Edmonton

NOR

Semipalatinsk

Irkutsk

Ulaanbaatar

MONGOLIA

Manchuria

Port
Sovetskaya Gavan'

Sakhalin

Vladivostok
Najin
Rashodate

Vancouver
Victoria

Seattle

Regina

SIN-KIANG

Urumchi

Ulaan

INNER
MONGOL

Gobi

Haerhpin

Changchun

Kirin

Shenyang

Seoul

Sea of
Japan

Portland

Salt Lake City

UNI

KASHMIR
Islamabad

TIBET

Lhasa

Lanchow

Peking
Tientsin

CHINA
Wuhan

Nanking

Tokyo
Yokohama

Yokohama to Vancouver 4244

Vancouver 4340

San Francisco

Colo

Delhi
Lucknow
Agra

Kathmandu

Chungking

Yangtze

Shanghai

Nagasaki

Int.D.Line 1380

International Date Line

Yokohama to San Francisco 4536

Honolulu to Vancouver 2430

Los Angeles

San Diego

Guaymas

Varanasi

INDIA

Calcutta

BURMA

Kunming

Foochow
Amoy

Ningpo

Taipei

Formosa
(Taiwan)

Canton

Hong Kong

(PEOPLES REP.)

Ogasawara
Gunto
(Bonin Is.)

Marcus I.

Tropic of Cancer

Yokohama to Honolulu 3380

Midway Is.(U.S.)

Honolulu to S.F.2100

Honolulu to L.A.2228

Tropic of Cancer

Revilla Gigedo Is.
(Mex.)

Acu

Bombay

Hyderabad

Madras

Bay of
Bengal

Rangoon

THAILAND

INDO-
CHINA

Hainan

China
Sea

Luzon
Quezon City

Manila

PHILIPPINES

Marianas

Saipan I.

Guam (U.S.)

Manila to Guam 1650

Guam

Wake I.

Honolulu 3387

Pearl Har.

Johnston I.

Honolulu

Hawaii (U.S.)

Honolulu to Panama 4710

Clipperton I.
(Fr.)

Trincomalee

SRI LANKA

Colombo

Nicobar

Andaman

to S.1530

MALAYS

Kuala Lumpur

Singapore

Ho Chi Minh
(Saigon)

BRUNEI

Sandakan

Mindanao

Yap

Caroline I.

Palau

Truk

Bikini
Marshall Is.

Washington I.(U.S.)

Palmyra I. (U.S.)

Fanning I.

Christmas I.

Jarvis I.

Equator

Maldive Is.

Chagos Arch.

Borneo

Tarakan

Sumatra

Celebes

Halmahera

Jayapura

EAST INDIES

Equator

Nauru

Banaba

Kiribati

Canton I.

Phoenix Is.

Malden I.

Starbuck I.

Caroline I.

Marquesas Is.
(Fr.)

Honolulu to Panama 6550

INDIAN

Christmas I.

Cocos Is.
(Keeling)

Jakarta Batavia

Java

Surabaya

Meluccas

Timor

Kupang

Bandjermasin

New
Guinea

Madang

Papua

Rabaul

Solomon

Santa
Cruz

Tuvalu

Rotuma

Tokelau Is.

Samoa

Tongareva
(Penrhyn)

Rakahanga

Manihiki

Suvorov I.

Caroline I.

Society Is.
(Fr.)

Tahiti

Tuamotu
Archipelago(Fr.)

Auckland to Panama 6530

OCEAN

Chagos Arch.

Tropic of Capricorn

N.W.Cape

Port Moresby

Torres Str.

Thursday I.

Coral Sea

NORTHERN

Townsville

TERRITORY QUEENSLAND

Darwin

Derby

Vanuatu
(New Hebrides)

Fiji

Suva

Tonga

Cook Is.

Tubuai Is.
(Austral Is.)
(Fr.)

Tropic of Capricorn

Pitcairn I.

Ducie I.

Easter I.
(Chile)

Amsterdam I. (Fr.)

Durban to Fremantle 4248

Durban to Adelaide 5100

Cape Town to Adelaide 5600

Geraldton

Fremantle

Perth

WESTERN
AUSTRALIA

Albany

SOUTH AUSTRALIA

Great
Australian Bight

Adelaide

AUSTRALIA

A. to A. 1040

Alice Springs

NEW SOUTH WALES

Canberra

Rockhampton

Brisbane

S.to FIJI 1750

S.to W.1280

Noumea

New Caledonia (Fr.)

Newcastle

Sydney

Lord Howe I.

S.to W.1270

Norfolk I.

M.to W. 1880

Auckland to Honolulu 3810

Kermadec Is.

Auckland to San Francisco 5700

St.Paul I.
(Fr.)

Cape Town to Hobart 5840

Melbourne

Tasman
Sea

Tasmania

Hobart

Bass Str.

M.to W. 1480

NEW
ZEALAND

Auckland

North I.

Wellington

Christchurch

South I.

Dunedin

H.to W.1250

Chatham Is.

Wellington to Rio de Janeiro 6980

Heard I.

Stewart I.

Bounty I.

Antipodes

Auckland I.

Campbell I.

Macquarie I.

PACIFIC OCEAN

Melanesia

Micronesia

Polynesia

Kaiser
Wilhelm II
Land

Queen Mary
Land

Wilkes Land

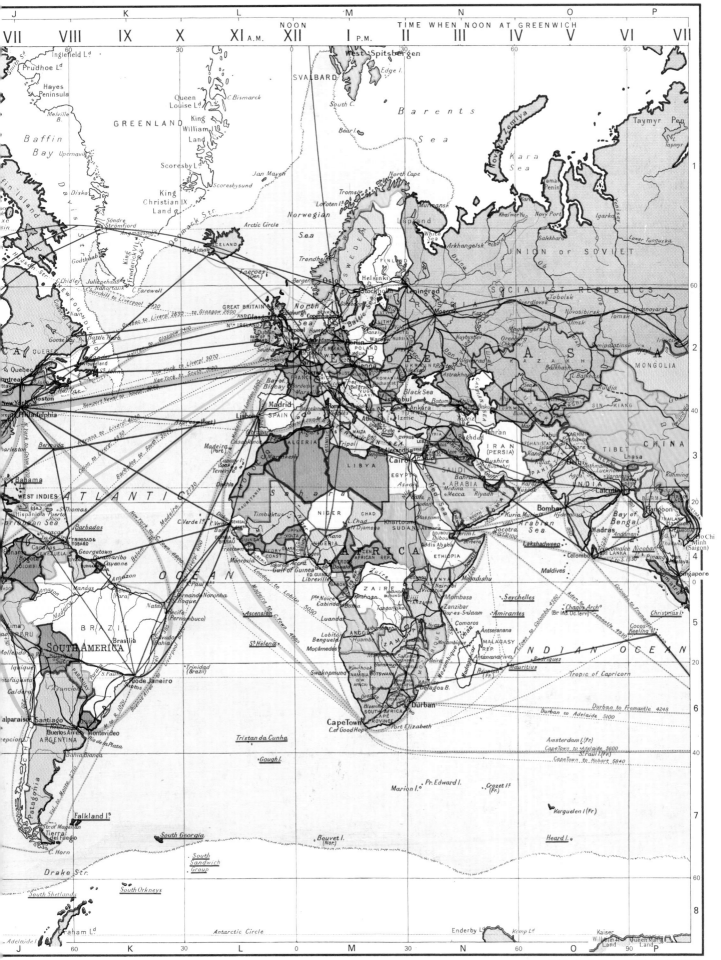

INDEX

This is a selected index, naming principal administrative divisions as scale permits, the major towns as well as many smaller places internationally well-known or having special local significance; and also including the names of major physical features.

ABBREVIATIONS

Austral. - Australia
B.C. - British Columbia
C. - Cape
Calif. - California
Can. - Canada
chan. - channel
Dem. - Democratic
E. - East
Eng. - England
Fed. - Federal
G. - Gulf
Gt. - Great
Hd. - Head
I./Is. - Island, Islands
Mt. - Mount
Mts. - Mountains
N. - North
Nat. - National
N.Y. - New York (state)
N.Z. - New Zealand
Pen. - Peninsula
prov. - province
Pt. - Point
R. - River
reg. - region
Rep. - Republic
S. - South
Scot. - Scotland
Sd. - Sound
Str. - Strait
Terr. - Territory
U.K. - United Kingdom
W. - West

Place	Map	Ref
Luton	4	F6
Luxembourg	10	E4
L'vov	10	G3
Lyme Bay	2	C7
Lyon	10	E4
Macapa	18	E2
Macau	12	O6
Macdonnell Range	19	D3
Macgillycuddy's Reeks	7	A5
Mackenzie District	16	E2
Mackenzie R.	15	E2
McKinley, Mt.	15	C2
Macquarie I.	21	C7
Madagascar	14	G7
Madang	21	C5
Madeira Is.	14	A1
Madison	16	H4
Madras	12	L7
Madrid	10	D4
Magellan, Str. of	17	D8
Maine	16	K4
Maitland	19	G10
Majorca	10	E5
Makasar Str.	11	O9
Malaga	10	D5
Malanje	14	D5
Malawi	14	F6
Malawi, L.	13	F6
Malay Peninsula	11	N8
Malaysia	12	N8
Maldives	22	O4
Mali	14	B3
Malin Hd.	7	D1
Malmö	10	F3
Malta	10	F5
Malvern Hills	2	D5
Man, Isle of	4	B3
Managua	16	J7
Manaus	18	D3
Manchester	3	D4
Manchester, Greater, co.	3	D4
Manchuria	12	P4
Mandalay	12	M6
Manila	12	O7
Manitoba	16	H3
Manitoba, L.	15	G3
Manizales	18	C2
Maputo	14	F7
Mar del Plata	18	E6
Maracaibo	18	C1
Maramba	14	E6
Maree, L.	5	C3
Marianas	21	C4
Marmara, Sea of	9	G4
Marquesas Is.	21	F5
Marrakech	14	B1
Marseille	10	E4
Marshall Is.	21	D4
Maryborough	19	G9
Maryland (Md.)	16	K5
Mask, L.	7	B3
Massachusetts (Mass.)	16	K4
Massawa	14	F3
Matapan, C.	9	G5
Matapo Hills	13	E7
Mato Grosso	17	E4
Maturin	18	D2
Mauritania	14	A3
Mauritius	22	N6
Mayo	8	B3
Mbeya	14	F5
Mbini	14	C4
Meath	8	E3
Mecca	12	F6
Medellin	18	C2
Mediterranean Sea	9	D5
Mekong, R.	11	M5
Melanesia	21	C4
Melbourne	19	F10
	14	B1
Melville I., N. Australia	19	D1
Melville I., N. Can		
Melilla	20	C7
Memphis	16	J5
Mendip Hills	2	D6
Merida	16	J6
Mersey, R.	1	D4
Merseyside	3	C4
Messina, Str. of	9	F5
Mexico	16	G6
Mexico, G. of	15	H6
Mexico City	16	H7
Miami	16	J6
Michigan	16	J4
Michigan, L.	15	J4
Micronesia	21	C3
Middlesbrough	3	E3
Midway Is.	21	E3
Milan	10	E4
Mildura	19	E10
Milwaukee	16	H4
Minneapolis	16	H4
Minnesota	16	H4
Minorca	10	E4
Minsk	10	G3
Mississippi, R.	15	H5
Mississippi, state	16	H5
Missouri R.	15	H4
Missouri, state	16	H5
Mitchell, Mt.	15	J5
Mizen Hd.	7	B5
Moçambique	14	G6
Moçâmedes	14	C6
Mogadishu	14	G4
Moluccas	21	C5
Mombasa	14	F5
Monadhliath Mts.	5	D3
Monaghan	8	D2
Mongolia	12	M4
Mongolia, Inner	12	O4
Monrovia	14	A4
Mont Blanc	9	E4
Montana	16	F4
Monte Bello Is.	19	A7
Monterrey	16	G6
Montevideo	18	E6
Montgomery	16	J5
Montreal	16	K4
Moorfoot Hills	5	E5
Moray Firth	5	E3
Morecambe Bay	1	C4
Morocco	14	A2
Moscow	10	H3
Motherwell	6	E5
Mourne Mts.	7	E2
Mozambique	14	F7
Mukden see Shenyang		
Mull	5	C4
Munich	10	E4
Murray, R.	19	E5
Murrumbidgee R.	19	F5
Muscat	12	H6
Musgrave Range	19	D3
Muztagh Ata	11	K5
Mwanza	14	F5
Mysore	12	K7
Nafud Desert	11	F6
Nairobi	14	F5
Nakuru	14	F5
Namibia (S.-W. Africa)	14	D7
Nanking	12	O5
Nantes	10	D4
Napier	20	C3
Naples	10	F4
Narvik	10	F2
Nashville	16	J5
Nassau	16	K6
Nasser, L.	13	F2
Natal, Brazil	18	G3
Natal, S. Africa	14	E7
Nauru	21	D5
N'Djamena	14	D3
Neagh, L.	7	E2
Nebraska	16	G4
Needles, The	2	E7
Nene, R.	2	F5
Nepal	12	L6
Ness, L.	5	D3
Netherlands	10	E3
Nevada	16	F5
New Brunswick	16	L4
New Caledonia	21	D6
New England Range	19	G4
New Forest	2	E7
New Guinea	21	C5
New Hampshire (N.H.)	16	K4
New Hebrides see Vanuatu		
New Jersey (N.J.)	16	K4
New Mexico	16	G5
New Orleans	16	J6
New Plymouth	20	B2
New S. Wales	19	F10
New York, city	16	K4
New York, state	16	K4
Newcastle, New S. Wales	19	G10
Newcastle-upon-Tyne, Eng.	3	E2
Newfoundland	16	L3
Newry	8	E2
Niagara Falls	15	K4
Niamey	14	C3
Nicaragua	16	J7
Nicaragua, L.	15	J7
Nice	10	E4
Nicobar Is.	12	M8
Niger	14	C3
Niger, R.	13	C3
Nigeria	14	C3
Nile, R.	13	F2
Nîteroi	18	F5
Norfolk, Eng.	3	G5
Norfolk, Virginia	16	K5
Norfolk Broads	1	H5
Norfolk I.	21	D6
Norrköping	10	F3
North Cape, N.Z.	20	B1
North Cape, Norway	10	G1
North Channel	7	E1
North Downs	2	F6
North Foreland	2	H6
North Island	20	B2
North Minch	5	B2
North Pole	20	D8
North Sea	9	D3
North West Highlands	5	C3
North-West Territories	16	E2
Northam	19	B10
Northamptonshire	4	E5
Northern European Plain	9	F3
Northern Ireland	8	D2
Northern Territory	19	D7
Northumberland	3	D2
Norway	10	E2
Norwegian Sea	9	D2
Norwich	4	H5
Notre Dame Mts.	15	K4
Nottingham	3	E5
Nottinghamshire	3	E4
Nouadhibou	14	A2
Nouakchott	14	A2
Nova Scotia	16	L4
Novaya Zemlya	11	H1
Novosibirsk	12	L3
Nubian Desert	13	F2
Nullarbor Plain	19	C4
Nürnberg	10	F4
Nyasa, L.	13	F6
Oakland	16	E5
Ob, R.	11	J2
Oban	6	C4
Ochil Hills	5	E4
Odense	10	E3
Odessa	10	H4
Offaly	8	D3
Ogbomosho	14	C4
Ohio	16	J4
Okhotsk, Sea of	11	R3
Oklahoma, state	16	H5
Oklahoma City	16	G5
Öland	10	F3
Olympia	16	E4
Olympus, Mt.	9	G5
Omagh	8	D2
Omaha	16	H4
Oman	12	H7
Oman, G. of	11	H6
Omsk	12	K3
Omdurman	14	F3
Onega, L.	9	H2
Ontario	16	H4
Ontario, L.	15	K4
Oporto	10	D4
Oran	14	C1
Orange, R.	13	D7
Orange Free State	14	E7
Oregon	16	E4
Orinoco, R.	17	D2
Orkney	6	C1
Osaka	12	Q5
Oslo	10	E2
Ottawa	16	K4
Ouse, R.	1	E4
Ouse, Gt. R.	2	G5
Oxford	4	E6
Oxfordshire	4	E6
Ozark Plateau	15	H5
Pacific Ocean	21	D4
Pagalu	14	C5
Paisley	6	D5
Pakistan	12	J6
Palermo	10	F5
Palk Str.	11	L7
Palliser, C.	20	C3
Palmerston North	20	B3
Pamirs	11	K5
Pampas	17	D6
Panama	16	J8
Panama, city	16	K8
Panama, G. of	17	B2
Panama, Isthmus of	15	J8
Papua New Guinea	21	C5
Paraguay	18	D5
Paramaribo	18	E2
Parana, R.	17	E6
Paris	10	E4
Patagonian Desert	17	C8
Peace R.	15	F3
Peak, The	1	E4
Pearl Harbor	21	E4
Peipus, L.	9	G3
Peking	12	O5
Peloponnesus Pen.	9	G5
Pennines	1	D3
Pennsylvania (Pa.)	16	K4
Pentland Firth	5	E2
Pentland Hills	5	E5
Penzance	4	A7
Perth, Scot.	6	E4
Perth, W. Australia	19	A10
Peru	18	C3
Philadelphia	16	K5
Philippines	12	P7
Phnom Penh	12	N7
Phoenix	16	F5
Phoenix Is.	21	E5
Pickering, Vale of	1	F3
Pierre	16	G4
Pietermaritzburg	14	F7
Pindus Mts.	9	G5
Pisa	10	E4
Pitcairn I.	21	F6
Pittsburg	16	K4
Plenty, Bay of	20	C2
Ploesti	10	G4
Plovdiv	10	G4
Plymouth	4	B7
Plynlimon	2	C5
Poland	10	F3
Polynesia	21	E6
Popocatepetl	15	G7
Port-au-Prince	16	K7
Port Augusta	19	D10
Port Elizabeth	14	E8
Port Harcourt	14	C4
Port Moresby	21	C5
Port of Spain	18	D1
Port Pirie	19	D10
Port Said	14	F1
Port Sudan	14	F2
Portland	16	E4
Portland Bill	2	D7
Pôrto Alegre	18	E5
Portsmouth	4	E7
Portugal	10	D5
Powys	4	C5
Poznań	10	F3
Prague	10	F3
Preston	3	D4
Pretoria	14	E7
Prince Edward I. (P.E.I.)	16	L4
Prince Rupert	16	D3
Pripet Marshes	9	G3
Providence	16	K4
Puebla	16	H7
Punta Arenas	18	C8
Pusan	12	P5
Pyongyang	12	P5
Pyrenees	9	D4
Qatar	12	H6
Qattara Depression	13	E2
Quantock Hills	2	C6
Quebec, city	16	K4
Quebec, prov.	16	K3
Queen Alexandra Range	20	F4
Queen Charlotte Is.	15	D3
Queen Mary Land	20	H3
Queen Maud Range	20	F3
Queensland	19	E8
Quito	18	C3
Rabat	14	B1
Rainier, Mt.	15	E4
Raleigh	16	K5
Rangoon	12	M7
Ras Dashan	13	F3
Reading	4	F6
Recife	18	G3
Red Sea	13	F2
Ree, L.	7	C3
Regina	16	G3
Reindeer L.	15	G3
Reykjavik	10	B2
Rhine, R.	9	E4
Rhode Island (R.I.)	16	K4
Rhodes	10	G5
Rhodesia see Zimbabwe		
Rhodope Mts.	9	G4
Rhondda Valley	2	C6
Rhone, R.	9	E4
Ribble, R.	1	D4
Richmond	16	K5
Riga	10	G3
Riga, G. of	9	G3
Rio de Janeiro	18	F5
Rio Grande	15	G6
Riyadh	12	G6
Rockhampton	19	G8
Rocky Mts.	15	D3
Romania	10	G4
Rome	10	F4
Roraima	17	D2
Rosario	18	D6
Roscommon	17	C3
Ross Dependency	20	F5
Ross Sea	20	F4
Rostov	12	G4
Rotarua	20	C2
Rotterdam	10	E3
Ruapehu, Mt.	20	C3
Rub al Khali Desert	11	G7
Rudolf, L.	13	F4
Ruwenzori	13	F4
Rwanda	14	E5
Sabah	12	O8
Sacramento	16	E5
Sahara	13	B2
Saigon see Ho Chi Minh		
St. Abb's Head	5	F5
St. Andrews	6	F4
St. Bees Head	1	C3
St. Davids Head	2	A6
St. Etienne	10	E4
St. George's Channel	7	F5
St. Helena	14	B6
St. John	16	L4
St. Lawrence, G. of	15	L4
St. Lawrence R.	15	L4
St. Louis	16	H5
St. Paul	16	H4
Salem	16	E4
Salford	3	D4
Salisbury, Eng	4	E6
Salisbury, Zimbabwe	14	F6
Salisbury Plain	2	D6
Salop see Shropshire		
Salt Lake City	16	F4
Salvador	18	G4
Salween, R.	11	M6
Salzburg	10	F4
Samarkand	12	J5
Samoa	21	E5
San Cristobal	16	C2
San Diego	16	F6
San Francisco	16	E5
San Jorge, G.	17	D7
San Lucas, C.	15	F6
San Marino	10	F4
San Roque, C.	17	G3
San Salvador	16	H7
Sana	12	G7
Santa Cruz, Argentina	17	D8
Santa Cruz, Bolivia	18	D4
Santa Fé, Argentina	18	D6
Santa Fe, New Mexico	16	G5
Santarém	18	E3
Santiago	18	C6
Santos	18	F5
Sao Luis	18	F3
Sao Paulo	18	E5
Sao Tome & Principe	14	C4
Sapporo	12	R4
Saragossa	10	D4
Sarajevo	10	F4
Sarawak	12	O8
Sardinia	10	E5
Saskatchewan	16	G3
Saskatchewan R.	15	G3
Saskatoon	16	F3
Saudi Arabia	12	F6
Sayan Mts.	11	M3
Scafell Pike	1	C3
Scandinavian Pen.	9	F2
Scilly, Is. of	inset 4	A8
Scoresbysund	22	L1
Seattle	16	E4
Seine, R.	9	E4
Selsey Bill	2	F7
Senegal	14	A3
Seoul	12	P5